Fact Finders®

SCARY
SCIENCE

TOP SECRET
SCIENCE

PROJECTS YOU
AREN'T SUPPOSED
TO KNOW ABOUT

BY JENNIFER SWANSON

CONSULTANT:
DENNIS SHOWALTER
PROFESSOR OF HISTORY
COLORADO COLLEGE
COLORADO SPRINGS, COLORADO

CAPSTONE PRESS
a capstone imprint

Fact Finders Books are published by Capstone Press,
1710 Roe Crest Drive, North Mankato, Minnesota 56003
www.capstonepub.com

Library of Congress Cataloging-in-Publication Data
Swanson, Jennifer.
Top Secret Science : projects you aren't supposed to know about / by Jennifer Swanson.
pages cm.—(Fact finders. Scary science)
Includes bibliographical references and index.
Summary: "Describes various top-secret projects, including the Manhattan Project, Nazi experimentation, and
several others"—Provided by publisher.
Audience: Ages 8-12.
ISBN 978-1-4765-3926-3 (library binding)—ISBN 978-1-4765-5124-1 (pbk.)—ISBN 978-1-4765-5973-5 (ebook pdf)
1. Military research—Juvenile literature. 2. Military weapons—Juvenile literature. 3. Espionage—Juvenile
literature. I. Title. II. Title: Top secret projects.
U390.S94 2014
623.4—dc23   2013022096

Editorial Credits
Jennifer Besel, editor; Veronica Scott, designer; Marcie Spence, media researcher;
    Eric Manske, production specialist

Photo Credits
Corbis: HO/Reuters, 19 (top), NASA/ Science Faction, 13, National Nuclear Security Administration/Science
Faction, 7, STR/AP, 17; DARPA, 19 (bottom); Getty Images: Barry King/WireImage, 15, Douglas Miller/
Keystone, 25, Hulton Archive, 8, Popperfoto, 21; International Spy Museum, 11; National Museum of the
US Air Force, 27; Newscom: Everett Collection, 23; Shutterstock: Alexandru Nika, 28-29, Melissa Madia, 14,
PozitivStudija, 4-5, solarseven, cover

Printed in the United States of America in Stevens Point, Wisconsin.
092013 007769WZS14

TABLE OF CONTENTS

CHAPTER 1
A SECRET WORLD.....................4

CHAPTER 2
DANGEROUS WEAPONS...............6

CHAPTER 3
HIDDEN PROGRAMS....................12

CHAPTER 4
HUMAN EXPERIMENTS...............20

CHAPTER 5
SPIES AND SECRET MESSAGES......24

CHAPTER 6
SCARY SCIENCE.......................28

GLOSSARY.............................30

READ MORE...........................31

INTERNET SITES......................31

INDEX.................................32

CHAPTER 1

A SECRET WORLD

Deep in the shadows, under lock and key, a secret project is under way. Hundreds of scientists are involved. No one can know what is being created. If it gets into the wrong hands, all would be lost.

This may sound like the beginning of an action movie. It's not. Top secret projects are real. They've happened in the past, and they are happening now.

Top secret projects have ranged from building bombs to medical testing on humans. The scary science involved in these projects was kept secret at all costs. Even today some projects are the world's best-kept secrets.

CHAPTER 2

DANGEROUS WEAPONS

It was 1941. The world was deep into World War II (1939–1945). German leader Adolf Hitler and his Nazi party were trying to take over Europe. The United States had just joined the war. Leaders were looking for a weapon that could end it. President Franklin Roosevelt started a top secret project to build such a weapon. It was called the Manhattan Project.

The goal was to build the first atomic bomb. This bomb would be the most dangerous the world had ever known.

Great efforts were taken to keep this project super-secret. Scientists were split up across the country. They used coded letters to communicate.

After four years, the weapon was ready to be tested. On July 16, 1945, outside Los Alamos, New Mexico, scientists exploded the bomb. A huge cloud of gas blew into the air. Windows more than 100 miles (161 kilometers) away shattered.

People were terrified. They demanded to know what had happened. The government said an ammunition dump had exploded. People believed the cover story. But one month later the truth came out. In August 1945 the United States dropped two atomic bombs on Japan. The bombs ended the war but killed up to 220,000 people.

WHEN SCIENTISTS EXPLODED THE BOMB IN NEW MEXICO, A HUGE MUSHROOM CLOUD OF GAS BLEW INTO THE AIR.

OPERATION VEGETARIAN

The Manhattan Project wasn't the only secret weapons project of World War II. During the war the Nazis were experimenting with biological warfare, a way of using germs to kill. To prepare against a biological attack, Great Britain decided to create its own bio-weapon.

THE BRITISH ROYAL AIR FORCE FITTED BOMBERS WITH TRAYS TO HOLD THE INFECTED CAKES. ONE LANCASTER BOMBER WOULD HAVE BEEN ABLE TO SPREAD 4,000 CAKES IN LESS THAN 20 MINUTES.

anthrax—a disease caused by a bacteria

Under heavy secrecy the British government conducted experiments with **anthrax**. In July 1942 the British military dropped an anthrax bomb over a flock of sheep. The sheep began dying within three days. Scary, right?

It gets scarier. The British decided that instead of using a bomb, they would attack the Nazis' food source. They created a project called Operation Vegetarian. During the project British scientists made anthrax "cattle cakes." The cakes were small patties of cow food filled with the deadly germ. When eaten, the cows would become infected with anthrax. If the tainted cows were eaten by people, the people would become infected as well.

By 1944 the British had more than 5 million cattle cakes ready to be dropped over Germany. But they were never used. On June 6, 1944, American, British, and other forces invaded Nazi-controlled France. The invasion pushed the Nazi forces back and eventually led to victory. Great Britain canceled Operation Vegetarian. All the cattle cakes were burned.

FACT:

EATING ANTHRAX CAUSES SEVERE STOMACH PAIN, VOMITING, AND DIARRHEA. BREATHING IN ANTHRAX IS ACTUALLY WORSE. ANTHRAX THAT GETS INTO THE LUNGS CAUSES SEVERE BREATHING PROBLEMS AND DEATH IN MORE THAN 80 PERCENT OF CASES.

INVISIBLE WEAPONS

The former **Soviet Union** had a group of secret police known as the KGB. The KGB's main job was to protect the country's secrets. But its other—**classified**—job was to steal secrets from other countries. The KGB used spies to gather information.

Sometimes the spies needed ways to kill people quickly. One branch of the KGB was charged with making spy weapons. One weapon scientists created was a poisonous umbrella. The umbrella contained a tiny pellet of poison at its tip. When the spy pressed a button on the umbrella, the pellet was released. The pellet was the size of a pinhead and caused a stinging pain in the person who was shot. But after three days, the victim died of a high fever.

Scientists also made tiny pistols that could be hidden in plain view. These pistols looked like cigarettes. But they were hollowed out to hold tiny bullets. The spy would pretend to light the cigarette, aim at the target, and shoot. It was an easy and effective way to kill.

Soviet Union—a former federation of 15 republics that included Russia, Ukraine, and other nations of eastern Europe and northern Asia
classified—top secret

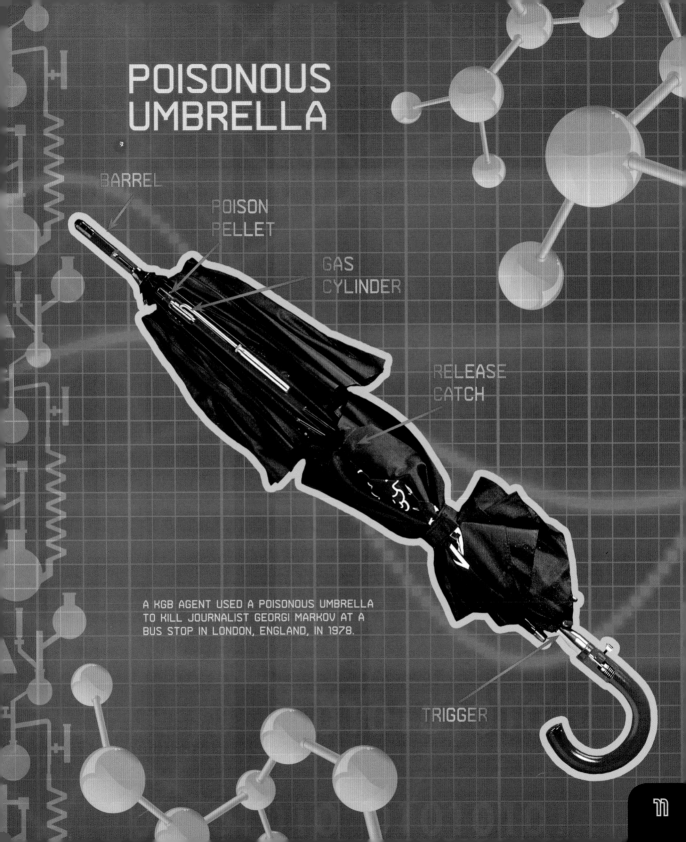

POISONOUS UMBRELLA

BARREL

POISON
PELLET

GAS
CYLINDER

RELEASE
CATCH

A KGB AGENT USED A POISONOUS UMBRELLA
TO KILL JOURNALIST GEORGI MARKOV AT A
BUS STOP IN LONDON, ENGLAND, IN 1978.

TRIGGER

CHAPTER 3

HIDDEN PROGRAMS

During World War II, Nazi scientists were close to creating the world's first rocket. The United States wanted that information. At the end of the war, a top secret plan was hatched to get it. The Central Intelligence Agency (CIA) would bring the Nazi scientists to the United States. They called the plan Operation Paperclip.

But there was a problem. These scientists were considered war criminals because of their work for the Nazis. War criminals could not enter the United States. CIA director Allen Dulles felt the technology the scientists had was more important than what they'd done during the war. Dulles had the scientists' background papers changed. The new papers said the scientists were forced to work with the Nazis. Then the scientists were secretly brought into the country without government approval.

Almost 500 scientists and their families were brought in during Operation Paperclip. Their work led to the creation of rockets, bombs, and **satellites**. It also led to the creation of NASA. But little else is known about the operation. Most of the information about the program is still classified.

THE NAME OPERATION PAPERCLIP CAME FROM THE PAPER CLIP THAT WAS USED TO KEEP THE SCIENTISTS' BACKGROUND PAPERS TOGETHER IN THE FILES.

MAJOR GENERAL H. N. TOFTOY (BACK LEFT) WAS THE COMMANDING OFFICER FOR OPERATION PAPERCLIP. HE WORKED WITH FORMER NAZI SCIENTISTS IN THE ARMY BALLISTIC MISSILE AGENCY.

satellite—a spacecraft that circles Earth

AREA 51

Disc-like planes fly overhead at odd hours. Flashes of light explode across the night sky. Strange humming sounds disrupt the still air. All of these incidents happened about 80 miles (129 km) outside Las Vegas, Nevada. They happened at a military base known only as Area 51.

Not much is known about Area 51. In fact, the government barely even admits it's there. So what really happens inside Area 51? According to documents released by the government, this military base has been used mostly as an aircraft testing ground. Spy satellites, **supersonic** planes, and even **stealth** technology have been developed there.

supersonic—faster than the speed of sound
stealth—the ability to move without being detected

SIGNS SURROUND AREA 51, WARNING PEOPLE TO STAY OUT

But some people believe the government is hiding alien spaceships inside Area 51. They point to the ultra-secret way workers have often been brought in. Workers were flown into the area on Monday and returned home on Friday. Area 51 workers were required to sign documents saying they would not discuss what happened there. If they did they would be jailed.

Many curious people have tried to find out what goes on in Area 51. No one has been successful ... and the government isn't telling.

BLACK OPS

The ultra-secret government projects that go on at Area 51 and places around the world are called "black ops." Very few people know what goes on in a black ops program. Every once in awhile, a bit of information about the programs leaks out. But since they are black ops, no one confirms or denies they exist.

The XB-37B is a new space plane owned by the U.S. Air Force. It is a 29-foot (9-meter) solar powered spacecraft. Launched in March 2011, it circled Earth for 400 days. What did it do up there? No one knows, and the Air Force isn't saying.

The RQ-170 Sentinel is an unmanned aerial vehicle (UAV). The first pictures of the top secret UAV were shown in 2007 as it flew over Afghanistan. The RQ-170 has been used to gather information on **terrorist** forces. It is undetectable by **radar**, possibly because of the material it's made from. The RQ-170 may be able to carry bombs. But it's black ops, so no one will confirm or deny it.

terrorist—someone who uses violence and threats to frighten people into obeying
radar—a device that uses radio waves to track the location of objects

IN 2011 THE GOVERNMENT OF IRAN RELEASED
PICTURES OF AN RQ-170. IRANIAN LEADERS
CLAIMED THEIR MILITARY SHOT DOWN THE UAV
AS IT WAS FLYING OVER THEIR COUNTRY.

DARPA

The Defense Advanced Research Project Agency (DARPA) is an organization within the U.S. government. According to its website, DARPA's mission is to develop technology for the military. But is that all it does? No one knows for sure.

DARPA does share some of its successes. Scientists there invented GPS and robot dogs. Right now they are working to develop a driverless car. Other possible projects include making a ship that is invisible to radar and **sonar**.

But a large number of DARPA's projects are classified as black ops. Security surrounding these projects is very tight. Not much is known about them. Some people think DARPA is working on a program called Project Pegasus. Project Pegasus is supposedly a way to travel through time. Others say DARPA is working to create super **organisms** that will eventually take over the world. Are these projects real? Who knows? Still, DARPA remains a great mystery. Perhaps that's the way the government wants it.

sonar—a device that uses sound waves to find underwater objects
organism—a living plant or animal

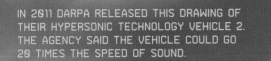

IN 2011 DARPA RELEASED THIS DRAWING OF
THEIR HYPERSONIC TECHNOLOGY VEHICLE 2.
THE AGENCY SAID THE VEHICLE COULD GO
20 TIMES THE SPEED OF SOUND.

ROBOT DOGS

DARPA created robot dogs to work
with U.S. Marines. These dogs are made of
metal and run on a gas engine. Each dog can
carry up to 120 pounds (54 kilograms) and
can run up to 3.3 miles (5.3 km) per hour.
The dogs can run, jump, and climb hills
like normal dogs. But they are run
completely by a computer.

CHAPTER 4

HUMAN EXPERIMENTS

Some of the worst secret projects in history had deadly consequences. Before and during World War II, the Nazi party, led by Adolf Hitler, tried horrible experiments on people. These experiments were illegal. When other countries found out about them, they worked to stop them.

In one **concentration camp**, doctors gave subjects deadly diseases such as malaria and tuberculosis. They used blood from the infected people to develop **vaccines**. Then the vaccines were tested on other prisoners. The vaccines had terrible side effects for some and killed many others.

In other camps doctors tried bone grafting experiments. They would remove the legs from one person and put them on another. Doctors wanted to see if a patient would survive the surgery. Most did not.

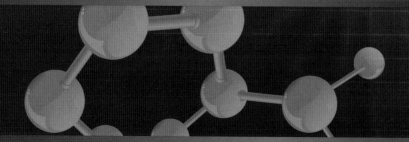

concentration camp—a prison camp where thousands of inmates are held under harsh conditions
vaccine—a medicine that prevents a disease

TORTURE

Other illegal experiments at the Dachau camp focused on ways for German Air Force soldiers to survive the war. The higher you go in the atmosphere, the less pressure there is and the colder it gets. Doctors forced people into low-pressure chambers and watched as they reacted. The people experienced swelling of the skin, sunburn, or maybe a pressure in the intestines at first. But after just 14 seconds, subjects passed out from lack of oxygen. Many died from this experiment. Others at the camp were frozen. Then doctors watched to see if the people could survive.

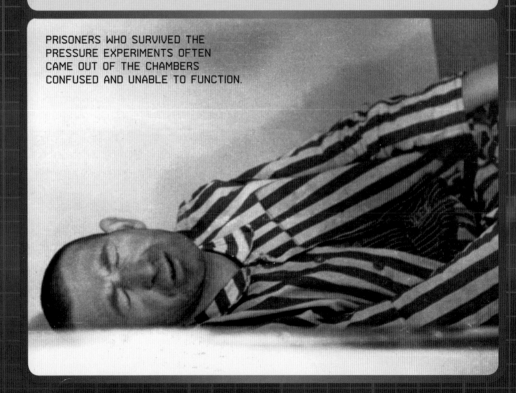

PRISONERS WHO SURVIVED THE PRESSURE EXPERIMENTS OFTEN CAME OUT OF THE CHAMBERS CONFUSED AND UNABLE TO FUNCTION.

MIND CONTROL

Project MKULTRA was all about mind-control. This operation was a top secret project created by the CIA. The goal was to find new ways to get information out of prisoners. Russia had used torture and mind-control techniques to get information from U.S. soldiers. The United States needed ways to do the same to Russians.

The CIA hired scientists at hospitals and universities to do mind-control experiments. But many of the scientists had no idea that it was the CIA that hired them. They were asked to do experiments to find out how certain drugs affected people.

Some scientists placed ads asking for volunteers for a drug study. People willingly took the drug. Then they told the scientists how it affected them.

But many other people were tested without their knowledge. Scientists or CIA agents held parties at their houses. They slipped drugs in partygoers' drinks or food. Then the scientists watched the reactions of the people. Did they become ill? Were they more talkative? Were they able to make these people do something they wouldn't normally do? All of the observations were recorded and reported to Project MKULTRA.

IN 1975 AN INVESTIGATION OF CIA PRACTICES FOUND OUT ABOUT PROJECT MKULTRA. PRESIDENT GERALD FORD WAS GIVEN A COPY OF THE INVESTIGATION'S REPORT.

The sad result from these parties was that many people became very ill. Some ended up in mental hospitals. One person even died before the project was shut down in 1970.

The information gathered from Project MKULTRA was used to create a CIA interrogation manual. This manual details questioning procedures. Parts of that manual may still be used today.

CHAPTER 5

SPIES AND SECRET MESSAGES

The best way to get secret information from another country is to use a spy. Spies are trained to communicate with secret codes. But when someone breaks that secret code, all secrecy is lost.

The Soviet Union was a friend to the United States during World War II. But that didn't stop the country from trying to discover America's secrets. Soviet scientists were hired to work on the Manhattan Project. But some of those scientists acted as spies. They sent information about the bomb to their home country through coded radio messages.

The United States found it hard to stop the spies from getting the information. Instead, leaders decided to figure out the coded radio messages. The U.S. government created Operation Venona. It took the United States two years to crack the codes. But when it did, leaders learned that the Soviet Union had gotten secret information on the atomic bomb.

The Soviet Union didn't know the United States had cracked its secret code. So U.S. agents kept listening. They were not disappointed. They were able to identify many Soviet agents from the information gathered in the messages.

A RUSSIAN CODEBOOK SPIES USED TO READ MESSAGES FROM LEADERS IN MOSCOW

FACT:

RUSSIA STILL SENDS SPIES TO THE UNITED STATES. IN 2010, 11 RUSSIAN SPIES WERE CAUGHT. THESE SPIES LIVED AND WORKED IN THE COUNTRY AS CITIZENS. BUT THEY WERE USING FAKE NAMES AND TRYING TO GET GOVERNMENT SECRETS.

SPY SATELLITES

Spies are great for collecting bits of information. But spies are human. And humans can get caught. Spy satellites are another top secret tool countries use to find out what's going on. Simply explained, scientists put high-tech cameras on satellites and send them into orbit around Earth. People on the ground send radio signals up to the satellites, telling them where to point the cameras. Satellites can be used to watch any place or person. And no one knows what or who is being watched.

The first U.S. spy satellite was called GAMBIT. It was part of a highly classified program that ran from July 1963 to April 1984. The GAMBIT satellite took pictures of Russia, Eastern Europe, and Asia. The United States wanted information on the sizes and strengths of the militaries of those regions. GAMIBT's long-range camera was perfect for the job.

A new, longer-range satellite was launched in June 1971. It was called HEXAGON. The HEXAGON satellite had two cameras that swept back and forth, taking pictures. The camera's film was then sent back inside four return capsules. Military airplanes captured the capsules mid-air and brought them back for research. The satellite was used to take pictures of Russia's submarine bases and missile silos.

Spy satellites are still in use today. New satellites track smaller targets and provide more in-depth information. Satellites such as the Lacrosse and Ikonos-2 were used to look for terrorists in Iraq and Afghanistan.

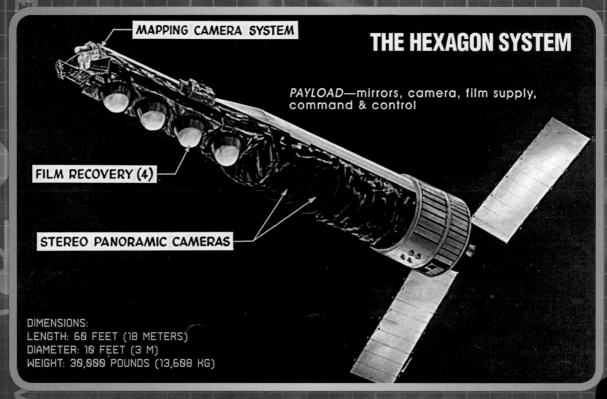

THE HEXAGON SYSTEM

MAPPING CAMERA SYSTEM

PAYLOAD—mirrors, camera, film supply, command & control

FILM RECOVERY (4)

STEREO PANORAMIC CAMERAS

DIMENSIONS:
LENGTH: 60 FEET (18 METERS)
DIAMETER: 10 FEET (3 M)
WEIGHT: 30,000 POUNDS (13,608 KG)

CHAPTER 6

SCARY SCIENCE

Germ-filled bombs. Cigarette guns. Parties where people are drugged. It sounds like a bad spy movie, doesn't it?

Real top secret government projects have been around for many years. More are created every day. Every government around the world keeps its secrets hidden and locked up. Who knows what scary science is happening behind those closed doors?

GLOSSARY

anthrax (AN-thrax)—a disease caused by bacteria

classified (KLAH-suh-fide)—top secret

concentration camp (kahn-suhn-TRAY-shuhn KAMP)—a prison camp where thousands of inmates are held under harsh conditions

organism (OR-guh-niz-uhm)—a living plant or animal

radar (RAY-dar)—a device that uses radio waves to track the location of objects

satellite (SAT-uh-lite)—a spacecraft that circles Earth; satellites gather and send information

sonar (SOH-narr)—a device that uses sound waves to find underwater objects

Soviet Union (SOH-vee-et YOON-yuhn)—a former federation of 15 republics that included Russia, Ukraine, and other nations of eastern Europe and northern Asia

stealth (STELTH)—the ability to move without being detected

supersonic (soo-pur-SON-ik)—faster than the speed of sound

terrorist (TER-uhr-ist)—someone who uses violence and threats to frighten people into obeying

vaccine (vak-SEEN)—a medicine that prevents a disease

READ MORE

De Winter, James. *Amazing Tricks of Real Spies.* Extreme Explorations! Mankato, Minn.: Capstone Press, 2010.

Martin, Ted. *Area 51.* The Unexplained. Minneapolis: Bellwether Media, 2012.

Vander Hook, Sue. *The Manhattan Project.* Essential Events. Edina, Minn.: ABDO Pub., 2011.

INTERNET SITES

FactHound offers a safe, fun way to find Internet sites related to this book. All of the sites on FactHound have been researched by our staff.

Here's all you do:

Visit *www.facthound.com*

Type in this code: 9781476539263

Check out projects, games and lots more at
www.capstonekids.com

INDEX

anthrax, 9
Area 51, 14–15, 16
atomic bomb, 5, 6–7, 24

bio-weapons, 8–9, 28
black ops, 16, 18

Central Intelligence Agency
    (CIA), 12, 22–23

Defense Advanced Research
    Project Agency (DARPA),
    18, 19

Hitler, Adolf, 6, 20

KGB spies, 10

Manhattan Project, 6–7, 8, 24

Nazi party, 6, 8, 9, 12, 20
    concentration camp
    experiments, 20–21

Operation Paperclip, 12, 13
Operation Vegetarian, 8–9
Operation Venona, 24–25

Project MKULTRA, 22–23, 28

spies, 10, 24–25, 26
spy satellites, 26–27
spy weapons
    cigarette pistols, 10, 28
    poisonous umbrella, 10

World War II, 6–7, 8–9, 12,
    20–21, 24